Change Your Life
With Self-Confidence

Introducing
The Confidence Method

Elisa Boogaerts

Woodhouse Publishing

ISBN: 978-1-989849-22-4

Designs by Amy Louise Baker and Elisa Boogaerts

Praise for The Confidence Method

"The Confidence Method is an invaluable framework to help us get clarity on who we are and what we want, so we can experience freedom in our lives to make change and ultimately be more happy."

- Kate Kuzemka

"One of the most significant learnings I got from The Confidence Method is knowing how to reduce my stress levels by doing breathing exercises, meditating and saying affirmations. I've been managing my stress and sleeping better as a result.

 - Eric Fish

Dedication

To all who want to
create a fulfilled life
and are ready to confidently
be themselves.
Now's your time!

Introduction

Back in the early 2000s, I felt stuck. Though really I was secretly stuck because my life seemed great and I felt like a brat for wanting to complain about it. Everything was "fine" but that wasn't good enough for me. I knew what I wanted but it meant change. It meant going against the status quo and all of the "shoulds" of life that I was already ticking the boxes of "like a good girl". The thought of uprooting my life to actually start living my life the way I wanted to was scary. But you know what, I did it anyway!

Fast forward 10 years, and I'm at rock bottom. I'm feeling the weight of depression, I have no money, I'm heart broken, I just moved to London England so everything was unfamiliar, I didn't have a job, and I didn't really know anyone locally. From here is where I was able to do a deep dive into all the areas of my life and decide who I wanted to be and how I wanted to show up in the world. I made the changes necessary to live to my values and what was truly important to me.

And then fast forward another 10 years and I'm feeling miserable in a particular part of my life. At the time, I had money in the bank, healthy conscious relationships and a home I loved but something was missing. I had to think about what I wanted on my personal development journey.

In life there are so many ups and downs. I would feel confident, happy and in flow and then life would take a turn and I wouldn't feel confident at all, nothing seemed to be going right and I felt lost.

When I was introduced to coaching, I saw the power in it and I was sparked! I realized that this was the missing piece. I found my passion to help people with self-confidence. I think it's the foundation for creating a fulfilled life. From a place of self-confidence is where you can go after what you want!

People perceived me as being confident and this is something I was proud of even though some of the time I didn't feel that way.

So I thought about how I've become confident. On this rollercoaster of my life's journey, I realized that I developed a huge toolkit of ways to increase my self-confidence so I could achieve my goals and what I wanted out of my life.

From this, I created The Confidence Method so I could coach my clients on these skills and be there to help them go after what they want with confidence. This book is that method. I'll take you through the 10-steps system to help you build your self-confidence, get to know yourself better, understand how you get in your own way of having what you want and how to deal with other people who may get in your way too.

I never want anyone to be stumped by that question - What Do You Want - like I was back in London. I never want anyone to be miserable in their life, like I was 20 years ago. I never want anyone to actually know what they want to do but not have the confidence to go after it. So I've made it my mission to help people with that.

May this book be that for you.

Table of Contents

Acknowledgements

Without knowing it, the creation of The Confidence Method, and hence this book, has been a lifelong journey. I want to thank my incredible family and wonderful friends for supporting me as I fumbled through life trying to sort myself out. Without them believing in me, their kindness, love and support, I wouldn't be where I am today and this book wouldn't exist.

I want to thank the Health Coach Institute and their amazing founders Carey Peters and Stacey Morgenstern for creating a coaches training program that launched my coaching career, my business and sparked my passion for coaching on confidence.

To my HCI coaches Alan Roby, Lisa Zaras, Kari Morin and Miranda Mitchell for their wisdom, for holding my hand when I needed support, for showing me my mirror when I couldn't see my greatness and for believing in me non-stop.

To Jennifer Grace for giving me the idea and encouragement to write a book. And to Kelly Falardeau and Kimberly Crowe for making it happen and getting me published.

1

Confirm Your Desires

Be you, confidently.

Welcome to Step 1 of The Confidence Method! In this chapter, we will explore how to confirm your deepest desires and discover your true motivation and vision of your confidence. This is just the beginning of your self-confidence journey and I'm so excited to get started with you!

Self-confidence is all about understanding your strengths and abilities, having a clear vision of what you want to achieve, and taking action to make it happen. It's important to remember that everyone has unique desires and motivations that drive them. What is it that you truly want to achieve, and why is it important to you?

Sometimes we can lose sight of these desires due to societal expectations, past experiences, or negative self-talk. But by acknowledging and embracing our true desires, we can start to build a foundation for authentic self-confidence.

Confirming your desires is the first step in building self-confidence because it gives you a clear sense of direction and purpose. It allows you to set goals that are meaningful and aligned with your values, which in turn gives you a sense of satisfaction and fulfillment as you work towards achieving them.

Consider this paradigm:

Nothing will change in your life
until you change.
Transformation to a confident life
starts with you.

To begin, take a moment to reflect and ask yourself the following questions:

- What do you want your confidence in yourself to look like within the next 6-12 months?
- What would you be able to do?
- What do I truly desire?
- What do I want to achieve or experience?
- Reflect on your past experiences: Think about the times in your life when you felt happiest, most fulfilled, or most proud of yourself. What were you doing during those times? What qualities or skills were you using? What values were you embodying? These can be clues to what you want to achieve in the future.

- Is there something that you've always wanted to do but put it on the back burner?

- Brainstorm: Take some time to brainstorm different ideas and possibilities for what you want to achieve. Don't censor yourself or worry about whether your ideas are practical or realistic at this stage. Just let your imagination run wild.

Would you play with me for a moment? Close your eyes for a moment, feel your feet on the floor, and take a deep breath in. Imagine a future version of you who is already experiencing what you truly desire. It's 12 months from now, you've achieved everything you set out to achieve. What does that feel like?

Good job! I hope that felt amazing!

Your Goals & True Motivation

Let's take this one step further and assess the authenticity of these desires. Are these desires truly yours, or are they influenced by external factors such as societal norms or family expectations? If you find that some of your desires don't align with your authentic self, don't be afraid to let them go and replace them with ones that do.

Take as much time as you need for this. Now, can you create a goal or two for this?

These are what we're going to be focusing on throughout this book. We will discover ways to increase your self-confidence so that you can achieve these goals. Creating clear goals will set you up for inevitable success. Write 1 sentence for what it is that you want.

Remember that this is a goal for right now and it may seem like it's not possible to achieve right now but we are going to work on your confidence so that you can go after it and have what you want! This is all about making positive changes or even small shifts in your life so that you can be happier.

My goals for the next 12 months are:

_____

_____

_____

_____

_____

These are awesome! Great job!

Let's dig a little deeper. What is your true motivation for wanting the goals you just wrote? What is the deep-down thing that is driving you to want this? One way to identify this is to ask yourself why five times.

Once you've gotten down to your true motivation, ask yourself, on a scale of 1-10 how important is this? If it's anything lower than an 8, you may want to reevaluate this goal or pick one that you really really want!

Connecting to your
True Motivation

Now that you have identified your true motivation we want to anchor it in. I want you to find something physical in your environment that you can connect with so it will remind you of why you're going after this goal, why you're making this effort and how important it is to you.

Anchoring in your true motivation can help you to keep making progress towards your goals, especially when you just don't feel like it or those negative inner voices tell you the opposite. Over time this is bound to come up! It's gonna happen, let's be honest. Know that this is OK! No shame or guilt is necessary.

A lot of your progress is going to happen outside of reading this book so these items will be like your accountability Confidence Coach. Little reminders to help you make conscious choices rather than defaulting to old behaviors and thinking patterns.

This will do two things. It will be a pattern interrupter—something that stops when you're tempted to make a choice or going into a negative spiral which may not be in alignment with your goals. These can help prevent us from making contradictory choices for ourselves.

So, think of some physical objects that relate to your 5 senses (sound, smell, sight, taste, touch) in your environment that you can connect with to remind you of your true motivation and your goals. What's something you can think of?

One of my goals is to meditate each day for 10 minutes. My anchor for this is a picture that I have on the wall of my bedroom. So when my alarm goes off and I want to hit snooze, I see the picture and it reminds me of my goal and my true motivation behind wanting to meditate. This is what gets me out of bed and onto the cushion, instead of pressing snooze.

My anchors are:

_____

_____

_____

This is great! Looks like you have some solid anchors!

Remember, the process of confirming your desires is not a one-time event. It's an ongoing process of self-discovery and self-reflection. Your desires may change over time as you grow and evolve as a person. The important thing is to stay connected to your desires and to continue taking action toward them.

Confirming your desires is a crucial step in increasing self-confidence. By acknowledging and embracing your unique desires, assessing their authenticity, creating goals, and knowing your true motivation behind them, and how to anchor them in, you can build a foundation for your self-confidence and begin your journey towards a more fulfilling life.

Actions

1. Start connecting with anchors and reciting your true motivation. Really make them mean something! Notice when you make choices that are not in alignment with this promise to yourself. No need to judge it, approach it compassionately and consciously. Every time you see, touch, or hear this item, it's a moment of truth: "Am I making the best choice for myself in this moment?"

2. Start working on your goals

3. Journal on this prompt: What will make all the difference in the world to me is...

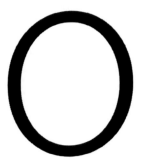

2

Organize Yourself

I focus on one thing at a time.

Now that you know your goals, let's figure out how to make it all happen. How to organize your life around all of the transformations you will be doing. There's a saying that "Nothing Changes If Nothing Changes". So let's make sure that change can happen because you are allowed to reinvent yourself and this is what this book is all about!

One of my superpowers is being an organized planner person which has helped me so much to achieve so many things I've wanted in my life so I'd like to share my superpower with you today to help you achieve your goals. I also find that planning really helps with burnout too.

Here are 4 ways to organize yourself:

- Set up systems
- Schedule it in
- Set reminders
- Master single-tasking

Set up systems

Setting up mini-systems for everything helps you to be super-efficient and reduces stress. This is especially important with something new. Create a system for it to make doing this new thing efficient and stress-free. For example, I have a min-system for when I get home. There's a shoe rack, a coat rack, a purse hook, a bench with a dish on top for keys, a bin for headphones and any accessories. So this is the order in which I do things when I first walk in the door. I throw the keys in the tray, take my shoes off, hang up my purse, take my coat off, take my headphones off and put them in the tray. So when I go to leave everything is right at the door ready to go. I never waste time running around in a panic looking for my keys like I know so many people do. I got my system, I'm good!

Schedule it in

This means putting everything in my calendar right away and keeping it up to date, always. Whenever you need to do something or commit to something or make an appointment, schedule it in your calendar immediately! If something gets rescheduled, update our calendar immediately. When you know what your schedule looks like, you can plan your time more efficiently.

Set reminders

Every time you think of something you have to do, put it in your phone with a reminder for when you need to do it or when it's due. This way you won't miss a thing! You can use a task app, reminders app or your calendar.

Master single-tasking

This is focusing on one thing at a time and completing it. Context switching has been proven to be inefficient because it ends up taking you more time to do all the things. When you stop a task and context switch to something different and come back to the first task, it can take up to 20 minutes to get your mind back to the place where you left off. There have been times when I've half done several things and maybe only gotten back to some of them which means that things didn't get done. A couple of ways to stay focused is to put your phone on Do Not Disturb so you won't have any distractions and to set a timer so you can focus on a task for a set amount of time. When the timer goes off, assess if you need to continue focusing on the task at hand or move on to the next task.

Take a look at your goals and see if you can create a system for one of them. You already created a system to keep you motivated by knowing your true motivation for your goals and having an anchor that will remind you of your true motivation so you'll continue to do the work you need to do to achieve your goals.

You'll need to create mini-systems for all your goals to set you up for success!

Let's start with your first goal. Break down this goal into smaller, manageable steps that you can take on a daily or weekly basis. Create a plan or a roadmap that outlines the actions you need to take to achieve your desires. And most importantly, start taking action today.

What's a mini-system you can create for it? What sequential tasks would be helpful for you to put in place now? Take a look at your calendar and see if you can start scheduling things.

Repeat this for all the goals you created in the last chapter.

Each step of The Confidence Method will have actions. Some things will be daily actions, some will be one-offs, some will take not much time, and some will take more time. How do you want to go about planning these? Go ahead, schedule it in and set a reminder.

Looking at the calendar you just created, how does this look? Does anything need to be adjusted?

Now let's think of a plan B if things change. You want to stay flexible but not become lazy. Think of a minimum that you'd like to spend on everything you just came up with and also a maximum because you don't want to take over your life. We're looking for change, not take over and sabotage! What would be a good plan B for you?

When starting to work towards a new goal or way of being, it's important to recognize, every day, what is going well with the progress you are making towards it. I like to think of success as each step that we take towards something we want, not just when we achieve it.

Sure, there will be ups and downs as you progress. Even in the downs, there is always something that is going well, no matter how small it may seem. All we're doing is recognizing ourselves for doing the best we can with what we have. Plan in time each day to recognize what you accomplished that day and give yourself a pat on the back! You are doing awesome!

Actions

Your actions for this chapter are to:

1. Create this plan for your goals and test it out. See what works and what doesn't work. For what doesn't work, adjust as needed and keep working at

it to make it work for you and your busy life.

2. Remember to set up a system to read a chapter at a time and do the actions - how can you fit this into your life.

3. Journal on this prompt: I am committed to shifting my relationship to time by...

3

Natural Mindset Shifts

*I take time each day to meditate
and practice gratitude.*

Step 3 is all about mindfulness and making
natural mindset shifts. It's about having
peaceful positivity, an acceptance way of
thinking, getting in touch with emotions,

and acknowledging and then reframing limiting beliefs. It's being completely in tune with your thoughts, surroundings, emotions, and body. When you're being mindful, you are happier, calmer, more relaxed, and appreciative.

Sometimes we can get stuck in a negative rut where we feel nothing is going right and we can dwell on what's going wrong. Our negative thoughts can spiral and consume us which can turn into an unhealthy pattern. What we need to remember is that even when things aren't so great, there are still good things happening in the world around us and even to us directly. Mindfulness really helps with this. To acknowledge the bad and still see the good.

Mindfulness helps us to:

- Relieves stress
- Stay in the present moment
- Deeply listen to others
- Observe your feelings and energy
- Calms you down
- Raises self-awareness
- Increases focus
- Re-centres you to the here and now
- Increase confidence

There are several incredibly powerful tools to improve your mindset and mental health. The ones we are going to focus on in this chapter are breath work, meditation, journaling and affirmations.

Let's jump in!

Breathwork

Let's start with breathwork. Using our breath is a great way to reduce stress. The way we breathe has a direct and immediate impact on the state of our mind, emotions and nervous system.

The parasympathetic nervous system is also known as the rest and digest or the feel and heal response. This is the optimal state for our bodies including digestion, healing, reducing stress, creativity, and mental health.

The sympathetic nervous system is also known as fight, flight or freeze. This is our stress response.

The classic textbook example is that if a lion was chasing you after lunch, you wouldn't be concerned about digesting your sandwich. The sympathetic nervous system would act effectively to shut down digestion, direct blood flow away from the belly and out towards your arms and legs for quick moving and up to your brain for quick thinking. This is a brilliant mechanism in place for our survival.

On a physiological level, your body doesn't differentiate between a lion chasing you and your boss yelling at you or getting tense in a traffic jam. One is life-threatening. The other is not. But guess what? On a physiological level, they are the same.

Interesting right!?

When your sympathetic nervous system is activated, which is all day for most of us, even at a chronic low level, our parasympathetic is shut off. These cannot be on at the same time. If one is on, the other is off. My Health Coach instructor, who's been a coach for 20 years, has seen many people cure heartburn, IBS, constipation, and fatigue by regularly using the simple technique of breathwork.

When we are in a stressful state, if we consciously adopt the deep and rhythmic breathing pattern characteristic of the relaxed state, we fool the central nervous system. The brain says something like, 'Hey, I thought I was a nervous wreck, but I'm breathing like a relaxed person. I must be relaxed.'

When we breathe, it's important to use your diaphragm. When you picture a baby sleeping, their bellies rise and fall, this is the type of breathing we want to be doing all the time if possible and the type of breathing we want to move into when in a stress response to move us back to the parasympathetic state.

So go ahead and put your thumb in the middle of your diaphragm, which is towards the top of your ribs. And put your other hand on the top of your chest, near your collarbones. Breathe in and push your thumb out. You'll notice that the hand on your chest doesn't move. You'll also notice that you don't need to push your belly out to do this type of breathing either. It's kinda right in the middle. Now put your hands on the sides of your ribs. Your diaphragm is quite big so it is also there. When you breathe in, feel your ribs expand.

This is the type of breathing we also want to do when we meditate or do any type of breath work or just all the time really.

Let's do a little exercise right now to test this out.

You're going to count the number of breaths you naturally take in 1 minute. Know that there's no right or wrong answer here. Just count them and don't try to force anything.

Start a timer for 1 minute and start counting your natural breaths. Go ahead and do that now.

Make a note of how many breaths you took breathing naturally.

Now do another minute but this time take slow deep breaths. You'll breathe in as much as you can and even when you think you're ready to exhale, breathe in just a little more breath, sip it in. And then exhale slowly and deeply until it's all the way out. Be sure to use your diaphragm like we just talked about. No need to count this time, just breathe as deeply and slowly as you can for 1 minute. Put the timer on and go.

Ok, now we're going to do another minute of natural breathing and you will count your breaths again. Don't manipulate it in any way. Simply allow the breath to flow in and out as it naturally would.

K, start your timer and start counting. Are you ready? Go!

Now note how many breaths you took breathing naturally. You may have noticed that the 2nd time you counted your breaths, there were fewer breaths than the 1st time. Was that your experience?

Meditation

Meditation is the practice of moment-to-moment non-judgmental awareness. It's being present with things just as they are right now. It's being at peace with the current experience. It's the practice of intentionally paying attention to the present moment. We usually use a focus point of the breath.

Meditation has so many benefits, this is why I'm such a huge advocate for it. It helps to calm you down, relieve stress, and become more self-aware which leads to focus, it re-centers you especially when using the breath, it's also a form of self-control.

If you haven't done meditation before, it can be a bit tricky to get into. A client of mine was brand new to meditation and when he would listen to the meditations I would send him each week, he would fall asleep. We even did a meditation in our one-to-one session together and I saw his head nodding off about 2 minutes in! He kept practicing though and didn't give up. He practiced at different times of the day and eventually found what worked for him. Then he noticed that his mind wandered a lot during the meditation. I told him that this is perfectly normal and to not judge himself for it.

This will always happen with meditation. Our minds are built to think. The trick here is to notice when your mind has wandered off, note it as thinking or feeling and gently bring it back to focusing on your breath.

Journaling

Journaling helps to integrate everything you are learning and the changes you are making in your life. It helps you observe, understand and deepen your experience which allows new creativity and insights to arise. It also helps you to see all the progress you'll make in this program. It can give you interesting insights and help you think through things to give clarity. It also helps you stay committed to your goals.

In each chapter, you'll see a journal prompt in the actions. With journaling, I encourage you to read the journal prompt and then start writing a stream of consciousness for 5 minutes. Anything that pops into your mind.

The journal prompt for this chapter is: What I am most grateful for in my life is...

So based on the last chapter's lesson and learning to organize yourself, take a look at your calendar and see if we can start scheduling time for meditation and journaling. These can be done together and will take up to 15 minutes. The meditations are typically 10 minutes long.

Where in your day do you have time for these 15 minutes?

Great! Schedule it in and set a reminder.

Affirmations

Let's move on to affirmations. Positive affirmations are statements that you make that open up your mind to start transforming and enable that statement to become a reality. They help us to make natural mindset shifts over time. They are positive statements of how you want your life to be. They also help to transform negative chatter or narratives that we have into positive ones. They are incredibly powerful and really help when we are actively evolving and changing.

Some of the benefits of affirmations are:

- Transforms negative narratives
- Raises self-compassion

- Puts a smile on your face
- They are mindset changers!

At the beginning of each chapter, you may have noticed that there's an affirmation under the chapter title that relates to the step of The Confidence Method. You can use these affirmations to repeat to yourself several times each day.

What system can you put in place to say affirmations repeatedly throughout your day?

I find that these mindfulness practices we talked about today, when done daily, transform the narrative in your head to a more positive, self-compassionate one.

When you have a more positive mindset and internal narrative, you can achieve your goals more easily.

Actions

1. Practice saying affirmations: I take time each day to meditate and practice gratitude.

2. Create a meditation space in your home - a sacred space for you to meditate, journal and say your affirmations.

3. Meditate daily at your scheduled time. There are many free meditation apps out there you can use.

4. Remember to breathe with your diaphragm

5. Journal for 5 minutes on this prompt: What I am most grateful for in my life is...

4

Find The True You

*I love all of myself.
I love the person that I am and
I do not need other people's
approval to love me some me.*

Step 4 of The Confidence Method is where you're going to do some self-exploration and dive into what's important to you.

Here's where you're going to start building the courage in your own being - your beautiful, unique, authentic self.

Consider this paradigm:

Desire is a wonderful guide, showing the path towards your life's purpose.

This reminds me of something Oprah Winfrey said: "When you know for sure that you're on course and doing exactly what you're supposed to be doing, fulfilling your soul's intention, your heart's desire. When your life is on course with its purpose, you are at your most powerful. Although you may stumble, you will not fall."

You've already spent time thinking about what you want. So in this chapter let's focus on who you want to be. You're going to do an exercise later to go through some of this but first, I'd like you to think about what authenticity means to you. Spend the next 5 minutes journaling on these sentence starters:

- If I was the most authentic version of myself, I would...

- How I want to show up in this world is...

Amazing! I hope those sentence starters helped you get more clear on who you are and how you want to show up in this world. This will help you start showing up as the person you want to be in every avenue of your life. What this looks like specifically for you can guide your choices and leave you feeling more confident in yourself and about the steps you take to create these new experiences in your life.

A few years ago, I worked with someone who was at a crossroads in his life. He had a good job and made good money but he was living day to day with no real purpose. We were talking over lunch one day and I asked him "Well, what do you want?" He looked at me blankly and said "Elisa, I can't think of the last time I was asked that…" This broke my heart. I personally ask myself this question regularly. I give myself the time and space to think about it and then go after what it is that I decide. This man had never done that. He also wasn't sure who he was at that moment in time. So much had changed for him.

This can happen to all of us, so it's a good practice to ask yourself these questions. Figure out who you are now, your current values and what's important to you.

Find The True You

Alright, let's do an exercise called 'Find The True You'. In this exercise, you're going to connect to your values/qualities and discover what's important to you right now. Knowing these things will help you to live more authentically and confidently.

Review this list of values and qualities. Which ones do you resonate with? Which ones are you aspiring to embody? Circle or note down the values and qualities you have or want to have. You'll find more in the Appendix. This list is not exhaustive, so please add any values that align with you.

Self-Awareness	Passion	Courage
Learning Agility	Patience	Abundance
Commitment	Authenticity	Confidence
Determination	Tenacity	Faith
Competence	Kindness	Spirituality
Compassion	Focus	Drive
Strategic Thinking	Resilience	Service
Collaboration	Self-Love	Flexibility

Self-Compassion	Creativity	Openness
Groundedness	Trust	Strength
Self-Respect	Inner peace	Curiosity
Maturity	Stillness	Sincerity
Versatility	Honesty	Integrity
Generosity	Backbone	Boundaries
Discernment	Intuition	Optimism
Enthusiasm	Creativity	Fun
Self-expression	Joy	Calm
Aliveness	Humor	Connection
Accountability	Love	Freedom
Appreciation	Power	Gratitude
Wholeness	Harmony	Beauty

The second part of this exercise is to define what's important to you right now.

Below is a list of intentions. Read through them and think about your true authentic self, right now in your life. What's important to you? Circle or note down the ones that you think are important to you in your life right now. Again, this list is not exhaustive in any way, so please add any values that align with you.

You are choosing what's important to you, your true authentic self, not what should be important to you. Sounds good? K, go ahead and come back when you're done.

Financially successful	A successful communicator
Physically fit and healthy	A loving family member & friend
A successful career	Well-respected
Music, dance, poetry, writing	Well-traveled
Spiritually developing	Politically active
Being in nature	A successful business owner
A contributor to my community	An effective coach, mentor, teacher
A visionary leader	A creator of beauty
An adventurer	Well-educated

Take a look at these pages and what you've circled.

Go ahead and read them out loud saying "I am….(values/qualities) and what is important to me right now is…"

Beautiful.

Go through those intentions again, one at a time, saying them out loud but this time just notice if any one of them lights you up… notice which ones make your heart feel full, the ones that are really super important to you right now. Take your time.

Amazing!

So what we want to do is live our lives being authentic, doing what we want to do while living to our values and prioritizing what's important to us. Connect this exercise to your daily life. Try to increase the time you spend on activities that are the most important, interesting and rewarding. Try doing only things that are easy, effortless, enjoyable, meaningful, and contribute to what's important to you right now. Make these a priority in your life. Consider which ones would bring you the most satisfaction and joy, and which ones will have the greatest impact on your life.

Actions

1. Increase the time you spend on activities that are important to you, interesting and rewarding. Try doing

only things that are easy, effortless, enjoyable, meaningful, and contribute to what's important to you in your life right now.

2. Don't forget to meditate and say your affirmations.

3. Journal on this prompt: What authenticity means to me is...

5

Imperfection, It's Perfect

*Perfection of myself isn't possible. I
am perfectly imperfect.*

In this chapter, we're going to dig into your
inner critic, self-judgments and how to
transform them into self-love. This is step
5 of The Confidence Method where you'll
learn that your imperfections are perfect!

Perfectionism is the forever waiting game! It isn't actually possible to achieve. Even if we have a goal and we do it "perfectly", once it's achieved, there is always the next thing waiting to improve upon it further. Or we hold ourselves back because we say "Once I have this... then I'll be ok". Another reason we can be so focused on perfectionism is because we think that if we get it perfect, no one will criticize us.

A client of mine told me that perfectionism was such a blocker for her that she excluded herself from her friends and family, and she became anti-social. She was so worried about what other people would think that she decided to see no one to avoid the potential of being criticized.

The truth is, someone is going to judge or criticize you somewhere at some point. You can't please everyone because we are all so different and have different perspectives that what you see as perfect, someone else will not see it the same way.

And you will likely judge yourself even harder. This is where your inner critic comes in because our brains are wired to a negative bias. So we almost always jump to a negative thought first. That will always be there and what we can do is practice noticing it and going through it to the positive or to take action. We want to release any shame and old stories that we have. We want to be curious and observe our judgments so we can have more self-compassion which is empathy + action.

It can also be scary and vulnerable to acknowledge that you are not perfect or didn't do everything you meant to do or slipped up or struggled with something or feel like you failed.

This is OK and totally normal.

So in this chapter, we are going to do an exercise to move from a place of judgment to curiosity to self-love. This is going to involve a lot of journaling to grab a pen and paper and let's get started!

Judgment to Curiosity to Self-love Exercise

Think about the following questions and/or journal on them:

- What's an imperfection that your inner critic brings up the most?
- What would you like instead of that?
- What stops you from having that?
- What judgments do you have about yourself with this?

Thank you.

Let's consider that this judgment has a positive intention, that it genuinely wants something beneficial for you. What could that be?

It's important to recognize that judgments can actually teach us or highlight something. All of our negative thoughts have a positive intention in one way or another. Often, there's an unfulfilled need, a desire, or an aspect of our life that needs acknowledgement and your presence. When it gets ignored for too long, it resorts to judgment, hoping that it will finally grab your attention.

You're making fantastic progress so far. Let's move on to a different exercise that I learned from the Health Coach Institute to bring all these insights together.

Transforming Anger
into Love Exercise

This exercise has 4 parts: Anger, Fear, Request, and Love. I'll provide sentence starters and I want you to repeat the words to yourself and then complete each sentence.

We start with anger because it usually lies behind our judgments. Complete the following sentence and express your anger as if your inner critic were talking to yourself out loud.

"I'm angry at you for..."

Next is fear. Share your fear of what will happen if you don't change. Complete the sentence:

"If you don't change, I'm afraid you will..."

Now's time for the request. Think of an action, no matter how small it may be, that will move you towards change.

"I recognize that you want to live your best life. My request is that you
let go of _____
so that I can _____."

Lastly, let's focus on love. Complete the sentence:

"I love you! You deserve..."

Great job! Thank you for being open to trying this exercise.

Now, based on these new insights, consider which actions, no matter how small, are worth taking to bring positive change into your life.

What's a positive affirmation we could create for this?

Ya, that's it! Thank you for doing such an excellent job!

Actions

1. Practice your new affirmations.
2. Do the action you created in this exercise.
3. Meditate & journal each day. Here's your journal prompt for this chapter:

What would it look like to love myself fully? (try to write down what a day in the life of you "loving yourself" could look like) What is stopping me from living a day that looks like that?

4. When judgments come up or you're resisting an imperfection or your inner critic becomes loud in your head, try to catch it in the moment. Confront it. Get curious as to where it's coming from and what its positive intention is. Ask if this judgment is really true. Then ask what else do you know to be true. How can you flip it into something more positive, compassionate and loving? See if you can create an affirmation for it. So next time it comes up, you can stop it

in its tracks and switch it to your positive affirmation.

6

Deconstruct Worries

I mindfully acknowledge and silence the negative chatter in my head that might be preventing me from achieving what I truly want.

Life is full of challenges, and some of them can be overwhelming, leaving us feeling paralyzed with worry. However, it's important to recognize that these challenges can actually be opportunities for growth and transformation. Consider this idea: your challenges may be your greatest gift. If you shift your perspective, it can be life-changing.

As a coach, I've faced many challenges. One time, a client came to a session in a terrible mood, and no matter what I said, she responded with snarky comments and frustration. I was triggered and my fight or flight response kicked in. I doubted myself and my abilities. Despite this, I decided to shift my perspective and view it as an opportunity to learn.

By deconstructing my worries and exploring what I was fearful of, I was able to find the gifts in that situation. It made me a better coach and taught me to be more patient and understanding. That experience was one of my greatest gifts, and it's helped shape me into the coach I am today.

When we worry, we tend to get stuck in negative thinking, and it can become difficult to move forward. The key is to be willing to explore our worries, understand where they come from, and learn from them. It's okay to make mistakes, to fail, to stumble, and fall.

A fulfilling life will inevitably include struggles and failures. Instead of judging yourself for your failures, consider them your biggest teacher and greatest opportunity for transformation.

When worries arise, it's important to recognize that it's a message from your heart telling you to be courageous. This is a moment to grow, transform, break through challenges, and step into your personal power. Being okay with your worries and breaking them down to make them seem less intimidating is a skill that can be developed.

Let's do an exercise now that I learned at HCI. Grab a piece of paper and a pen. Draw two vertical lines to create three columns. Title them Define, Prevent, Repair from left to right.

Define	Prevent	Repair

I'm going to take you through them one by one. Starting with the column on the left, Define.

First, think of something you are worried about right now that you might fail at. Something that you want and all the fears associated with it.

Write down bullets for all of the things you fear will happen in the Define column.

Now, thinking about this potential failure and all the fears, complete this sentence starter:

"If I was the most confident version of myself, I would..."

In the Prevent column, write down what you could do to prevent the things you wrote down in the Define column from happening if you were the most confident version of yourself.

Now, think of ways that you could repair the situations if they did happen.

Brainstorm everything you could do and write them down in the Repair column.

Based on these insights, what decision would you like to make about this?
What small action can you take this week to move you closer to this decision?

What support do you need to make doing that action inevitable?

Awesome! You've now deconstructed your worries! You've written it all out, which is sometimes all that you need. And you have a plan in case anything does happen. You can use this tool again and again for anything that comes up in your life that you are worried about.

Deconstructing worries is a powerful way to overcome limiting beliefs, and self-doubt and build self-confidence. By identifying your worries, reframing them, facing your fears and taking action, you can achieve your full potential and live the life you want to live.

Actions

1. Complete the action you identified in the session and do what needs to be done to make it inevitable.

2. Journal on this prompt: Something I want to do but haven't yet because of fear is...

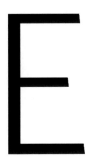

7

Experience Ownership

I practice kindness towards myself and others.

Part of being self-confident is being able to admit your mistakes and take responsibility for them so you can own your experiences while also being kind to yourself with self-compassion.

Owning your experiences means taking responsibility for your actions, reactions, and interpretations of events that happen in your life. It's about acknowledging your role in the experience and being kind to yourselves in the process. When you take ownership of your experiences, you shift the focus from external factors to your internal reactions and behaviors. You become empowered to make changes, learn from your mistakes, and move forward with greater confidence and self-awareness.

Consider this Paradigm:

Taking ownership of your experiences always leads to positive outcomes.

It is possible that you can admit your mistakes without beating yourself up or putting yourself down. Just because you made a mistake or didn't behave in a way that's aligned with your values doesn't mean that there is something wrong with you. You did the best you could with the behaviors you learned and now you're on a journey to become better.

Taking ownership of your experiences is not always easy. It requires you to be honest with yourself and to take a hard look at your behaviors and reactions. It also requires you to let go of blame, excuses, and victim mentality. This can be a difficult process, but it is essential for growth and personal development.

One of the keys is to develop self-compassion. This means being kind and understanding of yourself, even when you make mistakes or don't live up to your own expectations. It's about recognizing that you are human and imperfect, and that's okay. You can show yourself the same kindness and compassion you would show a friend who is struggling.

Another important aspect is learning to see things from different perspectives. When you can view a situation from multiple angles, you can gain a deeper understanding of your role in it. This can help you to learn from your mistakes and make changes to your behavior in the future.

Owning your experiences also means letting go of the need for external validation. When you are confident in yourself and your abilities, you don't need approval from others to feel good about yourself. You can trust your judgment and make decisions based on what feels right for you.

You can humbly do this as well. To be humble is to have or show a modest or low estimate of one's own importance. The beauty of being humble is that you can relax and feel comfortable in yourself because you're not constantly trying to prove yourself to anyone else. You know you, what you've accomplished, what you're proud of and this can be expressed but doesn't need to be outwardly boasted and bragged about.

This does not mean that you diminish yourself, make yourself small or put yourself down. You can definitely give yourself credit and talk about yourself with confidence but in a humble way. This liberates you from feeling inadequate by being able to express yourself freely.

I lived abroad for 11 years. During that time, I went on a self-growth journey where I lived up to my values and finally felt like I was living authentically. When I moved home, I found myself going back to my old ways of being. I got sucked right back into my old life. Some of the people I hung out with were not my people. I started working in an industry that was new to me and was not my passion. I was good at it but really, it was just a job for the paycheque. My work environment was a mix of amazing fun people and toxic bullies. I got right back into a dominant masculine energy, which was an old persona that I worked so hard to let go of. I got competitive with my running. I became insecure about my appearance. My self-confidence went downhill. I feel like I lost myself. All that I changed myself to be while I was away. The person I was when I was happy and successful in so many areas of my life.

I had to take a look at myself, my reactions, and my behaviors and be honest with myself to recognize that I made these choices. I said yes to going out with those friends. I said yes to the job. I didn't set boundaries at work. I chose to sign up for races and beat myself up if I didn't get a personal best race time. I chose to stop loving my beautiful body and let societal expectations dictate my worth. I chose to react in more dominant ways than to be kind and curious. The list goes on. It was from here that I could take ownership of my experience, admit my mistakes, and be kind to myself. From here I could make decisions that were more aligned with who I wanted to be, who I wanted to spend my time with, what I wanted out of my career, and how I wanted to love myself and my body. I also chose to be humble about my decisions. I didn't feel the need to prove to anyone that my choices and changes were just. They were right for me and that's all that mattered. I made plans and took action to live my life the way I wanted to. It took work and some difficult decisions but it was worth it.

To start owning your experiences, it's important to take an honest look at yourself and your behaviors. Consider these questions:

- What are some patterns you see in your reactions to certain situations?

- What part do you think you have in this situation that you can take ownership of?

- Where can you take responsibility for

your actions?

Once you have identified these areas, practice self-compassion and kindness with yourself. Remember, you are on a journey of growth and self-improvement, and it's okay to make mistakes along the way.

To sum up, taking ownership of our experiences is essential for boosting self-confidence. This involves being accountable for our actions, cultivating self-compassion, and looking at situations from various angles. By embracing our experiences, we gain the ability to make constructive changes, enhance our self-esteem, and become more self-aware.

Action

1. Journal on this prompt: Where can I show myself more self-compassion?

8

New Boundaries

I will do more of what makes me happy and makes me feel good.

Setting boundaries means communicating clearly and effectively about your values, beliefs, and limits. It's an essential part of self-care and helps you stay focused on your goals and well-being. By respecting and loving yourself, you create a positive environment for others to do the same.

However, it's common to face negative comments from people close to you when you try to improve your life. They may feel threatened and try to hold you back. It's important not to let their opinions influence your decisions or sabotage your progress for the sake of their acceptance.

The thing is, you can't please everyone all the time without betraying yourself. You need to remember that it's not your fault that they feel bad.

I remember when I started training for the New York Marathon, I had quite the reputation of being the person you call when you want to go out drinking. I was out a lot! This needed to change when I started training. I had to learn to say no and not feel as if I was letting people down by not being there to go out whenever they felt like drinking. I told them that I couldn't go out and why running this marathon was important to me. They did eventually understand.

So when you start making changes in your life, it may become clear that you may need to set some boundaries with those that you know and love. This can be as easy as knowing how to say 'no'. You want to say no in an honest, kind, assertive and respectful way. Saying no can be difficult so be sure to respond with a no as quickly as it makes sense. Delaying will just make it harder. When you say no, it's a good idea to give a reason and an alternative if possible. Another thing to keep in mind is to not apologize for saying no and be proud that you kept your boundaries instead of feeling guilty. You can say you are sorry to miss the event but not sorry for saying no. You didn't do anything wrong!

Here are some tips on saying no:

1. When someone asks for something from you that you don't feel comfortable with, e.g. lending money. Say "I understand your request, but I'm not comfortable with that."

2. If you've already got too much on your plate and someone asks you to help them with something. Say "I'll have to pass on this one. I won't be able to help out because I already have too much on. I need to give

myself time to rest and get my energy back." Another example could be "Thank you for thinking of me, but I can't commit to that right now."

3. A coworker asks you to cover their shift, but you have other plans or you are already too busy: "I appreciate the opportunity, but I'm going to have to decline." OR "I appreciate your interest, but I have to say no."

4. If someone invites you somewhere and you simply don't have time. Say "I don't have time to grab a coffee this week because work is so busy. Could we make a raincheck for next week? I can do Thursday" OR say "Thanks for thinking of me! It sounds like a lot of fun but I'm not able to go."

If someone gets upset by you saying no,

that's ok. You're not responsible for their reactions and experiences as we talked about back in the last chapter. When this happens, instead of letting them get to you, say to yourself "It's healthy for me to uphold my boundaries and allow others to have their experience of that."

Having a Difficult Conversation

Sometimes, to set a new boundary, you may need to have a difficult conversation with a loved one. What you need to do first is get clarity on your truth and what you need. Then think of how you can communicate this in an assertive and kind way by speaking your truth without needing to be right for everyone else.

It can be hard to speak your truth without worrying about the impact it will have on them and what they will think of you. You might assume that something bad will happen if you tell the truth but until you tell the truth, you don't know what will happen.

The moment you suppress the truth, you've already harmed yourself and the relationship. Withholding truth turns into resentment which leads to contempt. You may also harm the possibility of who you might become by suppressing the truth of who you really are. Then you end up living and projecting something that isn't true.

A client of mine told me that the difficult conversation she needed to have was with her son. She found herself constantly cleaning up after him. He was in his late teens and she felt that he was old enough to put his dishes in the dishwasher instead of leaving them on the counter for her. This drove her crazy and she found herself being resentful towards him. We practiced together what she was going to say, she built up the courage and had the difficult conversation. It worked! He started cleaning up after himself. This had a huge impact on her mental health and improved their relationship.

You can trust yourself and be loyal to your truth. knowing that your truth doesn't have to be right, it just has to be real for you. Self-love and self-confidence are honoring this.

Accessing your truth doesn't necessarily mean taking action. You can sit with it. Take the fear away. By saying it, it gives you space and then something starts to change. So let's take some time now to practice speaking your truth. Here's the communication tool I want you to use. It goes like this:

I feel_____ because_____.
I want/I'd like _____.

Think of someone who you have a withhold with right now. Is there someone you are not speaking up to and taking a stand for yourself that you have a need or a want?

Ok, great. Now let's use the communication tool to start coming up with what you might want to say to this person. Come up with a couple of different drafts of this. You may notice that the first time you write this out, you might be blaming that person or needing to be right or to prove that you are right and they were in the wrong. Keep practicing and see where it takes you. You may notice that your last draft is drastically different from the first!

It's ok if emotions come up too. Let the emotions flow through you.

Remember that accessing your truth doesn't necessarily mean taking action, so you can choose what you want to do with this. Sometimes just knowing what you want is good enough for you and from there you can make a decision. The other person may never need to know you did this exercise.

And of course, you can actually have a

difficult conversation with that person if you feel it's right. I know that you can do it! Remember all that you've learned in this book so far and the self-confidence you've gained. You can do this!

Action

1.   Journal on this prompt: What I am noticing about my relationship patterns is...

9

Cohesion

What I want, wants me more.

Cohesion is defined as the act or fact of forming a united whole. This is the 9th step of The Confidence Method where you will bring it all together and then you are going to align yourself with your inspiring future. This step aims to take all that you've learned throughout this book and see how you can apply it to your daily life. This book is designed to transform your self-confidence so you can love yourself fully and make positive change in your life.

With this new way of being, you can go after what you truly want for yourself in your life. The person you were at the beginning of the book will be different from the person you become at the end. We are ever-changing.

Knowing what you want will also have shifted so it's the perfect time to ask what you want now or what in your life needs nourishment and change.

In order to do something you've never done, you've got to become someone you've never been. You must believe that it's possible to turn your dreams into reality.

Say this out loud for me:

It's Possible!

You are not defined by your past or your current struggle but by what you are creating going forward. You want to feel fabulous in your life so you've got to start looking for ways to be an active positive force in that venture.

So I want to do an affirmation exercise with you now. Below is a list of affirmations and I want you to say them out loud. Take a second to get settled before you start by closing your eyes and taking a few deep breaths using your diaphragm.

K, when you're ready, say these affirmations:

- I focus on one thing at a time
- I take time each day to meditate and practice gratitude
- I love all of myself.
- I love the person that I am and I do not need other people's approval to love me some me.
- Perfection of myself isn't possible. I am perfectly imperfect.
- I mindfully acknowledge and silence the negative chatter in my head that might be preventing me from achieving what I truly want.
- I practice kindness towards myself.
- I practice kindness towards others.
- I will do more of what makes me

happy and makes me feel good.

- I'm learning as I go.
- I acknowledge my own self-worth
- With each breath, I breathe life into my confidence.
- I believe in myself.
- What I want, wants me more.

Take a moment to check in and see how you are feeling right now.

I know that these beliefs may not all have sunk in yet but they are possible and you may feel your self-confidence restored. You wouldn't be here if you weren't ready for an update on your beliefs.

Acknowledge all your successes, every single step, instead of demanding everything be perfect right now to prove that you're on the right track.

Big 5 Visioning Exercise

Overcoming the challenge of letting go of our past mistakes and imagining a brighter future can be difficult. It's easy to feel trapped by our history and struggle to move forward. However, I want to encourage you to see beyond your past and acknowledge the personal growth you've achieved. Give yourself permission to embrace your most radiant, aligned, harmonized, and triumphant self. Together, let's envision an inspiring future for all areas of your life by exploring the Big 5 and what you want for each of them.

The Big 5 areas of life are:

1. Health
2. Career

3. Money/Finances

4. Love/Relationships

5. Mindfulness or Spirituality or Religion

For each of the 5 areas, you are going to brainstorm 3 outcomes you would like for yourself in the next 12 months. Grab a piece of paper and pen so you can write these out.

Let's start with Health. Ask yourself "The top 3 outcomes I see in the next 12 months in my health are..." Start brainstorming what they might be for you. You could have only one or two but keep it to a max of three. No pressure to have all 3. Often if we want something for ourselves, we need to make shifts in all 5 areas of our life. Go ahead and write these down.

Alright, now take a deep breath.

Let's move on to Career. Ask yourself "The top 3 outcomes I see in the next 12 months in my career are". These could be one-word responses or could be a statement of response. Start brainstorming what they might be for you. Remember for these to be what you want for yourself, not what you think you have to have or do.

Beautiful. Take another deep breath.

Let's move on to Money/finances. Same question: "The top 3 outcomes I see in the next 12 months with my money or finances are". Start brainstorming what your top 1-3 might be for you.

Nice! Take another deep breath. All the

way in and all the way out.

Next up is Love/relationships. Ask yourself "The top 3 outcomes I see in the next 12 months in my experience of love are". Really let whatever comes up be what it is. No modifying or changing or analyzing if it's good or not so good or if it could be something better, just allow the truth to flow. This also doesn't have to be romantic, it could be to show love in any relationship you have. Perhaps you want to show yourself more self-love and kindness by improving your relationship with yourself.

Now, take another nice deep breath and we're going to move right into the last one which is Mindfulness or religion or spirituality. You could also think of this as mental health if none of those other ones resonate with you. The top 3 outcomes I see in the next 12 months in my experience with mindfulness are....

Amazing! Now, take a moment to review everything you've written down for the next 12 months in the 5 key areas of your life. Identify the top 3 goals that you want to focus on by ticking or circling them. You can choose from any of the areas such as health, love, career or money. There is no right or wrong way to do this. By selecting 3 goals, you can make the biggest impact on your day-to-day life. This doesn't mean that the other goals won't happen, but you are starting with a focus. Which goal do you feel most drawn to first? Circle that one. Then, identify the next one that you feel drawn to and circle it as well. Finally, choose your 3rd goal and circle it.

Fantastic, great work!

As we come to the end of this chapter, I suggest that you don't rush to take any action right away. Even though we often feel the need to act quickly, it's better to give yourself some time to think it over. See if any new ideas or perspectives come to mind. Keep these pages nearby and go over them daily to remind yourself of your goals and aspirations for the year ahead. When you feel ready, figure out the first steps you can need to take to achieve one of your goals.

Action

1.   Journal on this prompt: What my new vision is...

10

Evolution

I'm confident. I'm relaxed.
I love my life!

Oh my goodness! You made it to the final step of The Confidence Method! In this chapter, we are going to talk about your evolution and look at where you will go from here.

Let's start by reviewing all that we've gone over in this book so far.

Step 1 - Confirm Your Desires - you created meaningful goals, defined your true motivation and found items to connect you to your true motivation.

Step 2 - Organize yourself - you learned how to create systems, schedule everything, set reminders and become a master of single-tasking.

Step 3 - Natural Mindset Shifts - you were introduced to the power of breath work, meditation, journaling and affirmations.

Step 4 - Find The True You - you discovered what authenticity means to you. You did the Find the True You exercise to identify your values and what's important to you right now.

Step 5 - Imperfection, It's Perfect - this is where you learned how to love yourself, your imperfect self, and that perfection isn't a thing nor possible. You transformed your judgements into curiosity & self-love.

Step 6 - Deconstruct Worries - you deep dived into your worries and fears behind failure then defined how to break through those fears.

Step 7 - Experience Ownership - this was all about admitting mistakes, taking responsibility, self-compassion and what humble confidence means to you.

Step 8 - New Boundaries - you were given

communication tools for saying no and speaking your truth.

Step 9 - Cohesion - you did the Big 5 Visioning exercise so you can align all that you've learned with your aspiring future!

I wanted to take a moment to acknowledge all of the progress you've made! As you move forward, it's important to continually recognize how far you've come. So scan around your mind for what it was like back then and what it's like now. Notice all the things, even the little things, that have changed between then and now.

What are some things that you have initiated, accomplished or shifted?

What are you proud of yourself for?

What is something you had to learn or overcome to have these results now?

Isn't all that amazing? Look at what you did when you committed yourself to your personal growth and self-confidence. Even though you may be excited for whatever comes next for you in your journey, it's important to have completion with what you set out to accomplish when you started this book.

Transformation happens with progression, building on top of a solid foundation, which is what we have begun to create here. Consistency is key to building confidence habits that last. In order to catapult to the next level, we've got to seal in the differences that make the difference.

I'd like you to do a journaling completion ritual now.

What are some of the most influential life moments that you want to take with you from this book? Think of these as new ways of being, or identifying, when it comes to your confidence, mindset and lifestyle.

Take a moment to journal about them and come back to this page when you're done.

Confidence is ever-evolving. We grow, we learn, we fall, we get up. I've had times in my life where I was so great and everything was in flow and then something big happened and I had to start all over again. The best part was that I had the tools, the same ones you now have from this book, to help me get my confidence back and take steps forward into the next chapter of my life.

These tools are yours to have forever. Come back to this book time and time again if you need to.

I want to thank you so much for choosing this book to be part of your journey. I really hope that you can take all of the things you've learned and the new habits you've formed to help you progress even further. Always remember how far you've come and all the awareness you have of yourself now. Use this newfound self-confidence to follow your dreams and accomplish all those goals you created!
I wish you the best of luck with everything you do in the future.

Here are two final journal prompts for you:

1. What I learned about myself is...

2. Where I need more support in my life is...

Appendix

List of more values & qualities

Accomplishment	Flexibility	Meaning
Achievement	Friendship	Merit
Adventure	Fulfillment	Moderation
Autonomy	Genuineness	Money
Balance	Good Will	Nature
Challenge	Hard Work	Optimism
Clarity	Healing	Perseverance
Communication	Holistic Living	Pleasure
Community	Honor	Professionalism
Conservation	Improvement	Progress
Credibility	Independence	Prosperity
Decisiveness	Individuality	Purpose
Democracy	Initiative	Success
Diversity	Innovation	Timeliness
Education	Intelligence	Tolerance
Efficiency	Intimacy	Truth
Environment	Justice	Unity
Equality	Knowledge	Vitality
Excellence	Leadership	Wealth
Fairness	Loyalty	Wisdom

Resources

Thank you so much for taking the time to read this book. It was fun sharing my work with you and helping you become more self-confident. If you're looking for more information, resources, tools or to take the next step, please visit my website at: inspirationbyelisa.com.

On my website, you can also subscribe to my weekly newsletter where you'll get confidence tips, health tips, life lessons, freebies and info on upcoming challenges, events and programs.

I have a few free resources for you.

You can scan the QR codes to sign up.

The 4 C's of Confidence

If you want to learn more ways to increase your confidence check out The 4 C's of Confidence Video Series! At the end of this series your confidence will be boosted and you'll have some more tools so you can go after what you want in any area of your life.

5 Energy Tips

Feeling exhausted? Do you feel like you have so much on your plate with all the things you're supposed to do that you hardly have time for the things you want to do? These 5 tips are going to help you thrive in this demanding world we find ourselves in. By implementing these top 5 tips, you can boost your energy levels, start reclaiming your time, and experience a greater sense of freedom.

Looking to take the next step in your self-confidence journey?

If you found this book valuable and you'd like some more accountability and someone to help guide you each step of the way, join me for a Confident You Discovery Session. This 60-minute session is dedicated to you where you will discover what your vision is for your life and the confident you living it. You will:

- Create a sense of clarity about what change you want.

- Determine the main thing stopping you from going after it.

- Identify an action that will move you toward what you truly desire.

- Complete the consultation with the confidence of knowing exactly what to do next.

- The session is complementary and you can book it here:

About The Author

Elisa is a dedicated and passionate figure in the transformation movement. As the founder of Inspiration By Elisa and a certified Life and Health Coach specializing in confidence, Elisa is on a mission to empower individuals to make positive changes in their lives.

Elisa's dynamic and inspiring presence has captivated audiences at summits, podcasts, and YouTube channels. Her valuable insights have been featured in top publications like medium.com, Authority Magazine, Wellness Voice, and CBNation.

Her signature approach to confidence-building helps clients unlock their inner potential and develop a mindset necessary to achieve their goals. Whether you're feeling stuck in your career, struggling to find balance in your personal life, or simply looking for a boost in self-confidence, Elisa's unwavering commitment to your growth and success will inspire you to take action and realize your true potential. Join her on this transformative journey and discover the power of self-confidence to change your life for the better.

Manufactured by Amazon.ca
Acheson, AB

10757242R00085